A DIAMOND ASHANTI SHORT STORY:

HOME BREW IN JAMAICA

BY RUDY D'DUDE

ONRUSH MEDIA GROUP

DEDICATED TO THE BEAUTIFUL
ISLAND OF JAMAICA

SERIES 2

Previously on A Diamond Asanti Short Story……..

2 hours before the closing of the stock market, Mr. Diamond is on the phone talking with his lead stock trader Raymond Alexander, advising, yet, ordering him to buy European Government Bonds and a large block of Deiago's stock after it had dipped for the third straight week.

"Raymond, I respect your intellect, but right now I can care less, purchase it!"

"Spider, go handle that, you'll understand later. And go learn some Guizhou language and be ready to travel to China."- Diamond referring to his childhood friend's nickname Raymond "Spider" Alexander.

……..Diamond continues to build his empire.

Shupavu's International Portfolio:

27% Equity of Hotel Gortina Spa Resort

100% Equity of Pietru Awditorju

wall street trading talk, wall street trading talk, wall street trading talk, wall street trading talk ....

"another 500 thousand shares at 42 and a quarter ($42.25)!?!?!?.... deal... Oh yeah, and tell your cousin to stop hearting all my pics on Instagram. My wealthy widowing cougar is questioning me. Ha Ha Ha" – Raymond "Spider" Alexander

"Another 500 thousand shares at 42 and a quarter Spider?" – Desmond "Dez" Cosby

"We got it, Dez!"– Spider

Meanwhile, in Diamond Asanti's office, him, TD (Thomas Downing, the COO) and his real estate executive staff are having a meeting on how to purchase the beautiful island of Jamaica.

"Ladies and Gents, I want to touch it all. From West End to Runaway Bay to Duckenfield to Portland Cottage BACK to West End...... Also, ESPECIALLY, I want to create heavy traffic between south of Treasure Beach to the Accompong Maroon to the St. Elizabeth Parish. TD, what is the balance of the real estate fund?"- Diamond asked

"Mr. Asanti, it is up to a bit over 4.9 billion dollars..... Malta has been gracious within these last 3 years.... American, Asian and European Cruiseline Companies are calling with lease proposals to build ports on Shupavu's Estate? They see the tourism future of Malta."-Thomas responded.

"Uhm hmm, alright, team, we are going to do a bit over 10% of the real estate account, at or no more than $500Million...... Within all, our first step is to buy, then own, cultivate, modernize and bring prosperity within Shupavu and the community. LET'S GEAUX GET IT!" - Diamond spoke.

"Yes sir!" as the team break from the meeting.

Diamond, as always looking calm, and collect, lean back in his executive chair reminiscing of his father's stories of growing up in Accompong, Jamaica.

One particular very short but powerful story by Diamond's father, the famous Jamaican Chef Levi Lee Asanti, explained to Diamond about his decision of leaving Jamaica to attend culinary at North Miami-Johnson & Wales University.

"Son, I left Accompong because I WANTED the opportunity for the world to know Accompong, and America was my key. I had a goal, and I had to go obtain it. One life son."

Buzzing his assistant, "Kendra, schedule a meeting with TD, Spider, and Dez 15 minutes after the Close Of The Bell." Diamond

"Yes sir, Mr. Asanti"..... "Mr. Sarou Adeyemi of Sarou's Tailor and Custom Fit is here to meet you." Kendra responded

"Send him in" Diamond

After the stock market closing of the bell, Diamond met with his Trading Team.

"Ok fellas, how are we looking on the Deiago Brewing play?" Diamond asked his Trading Team.

"Time for us to file the 13D, Mr. Asanti. As of today, we are over 7% of ownership (10.5 million shares)." Raymond responded.

TD cleared his throat to get everybody attention "Suggestion, we have 10 days to file the 13D, correct?.... Let's make this play suspenseful." Thomas spoke and smirked at Raymond.

Diamond immediately smiled, "Spider, how is your Guizhou language coming along?" Diamond asked

"Oh yes, of course, the Maochow Koutai Company. They own 4% of Deiago's outstanding shares. And probably ready to sell them since the price has dropped significantly." Raymond surprisingly responded

TD excitedly shouted, "Today is Monday, we will need their block of shares by Thursday." Thomas then looked at Diamond, "permission to use the company's jet, for Wednesday sir?"

"You already know it is done." Diamond

"The price was at $42.88 at closing, where or how much we are going to buyout Maochow's shares?" Desmond

"Bottom line! I like that Desmond! Get straight to the point! How much are we going to buy them out at?" Diamond then stood up and begin walking away from his desk toward the team, "Gentlemen, Dez, and Spider, after you all leave this office, the strategy for the call option trade for Maochow's and Deiago's Stocks, need to be completed before or at 5 in the morning tomorrow. Matter of fact, get a couple blocks Maochow's stocks during premarket. Let's set and stir the tone like it is a Mayweather Promotion Fight…. A maximum return." Diamond chuckled while talking to his team

"Yes sir" Desmond shouted as stood up

"TD, no more than $51 a share." Diamond spoke to Thomas

"Sir, I was thinking $48.50 a share." Thomas responded with enthusiastic confidence

6:32 am, next morning, TD, Spider and Dez boarded the company's jet en route to China as if they were a discreet special operation force to execute a negotiated deal of "The Deiago Brewing Play".

"Mr. Downing, have you ever done a deal of this magnitude overseas like this before?" Desmond asked

TD looked over to Dez with a stern facial expression and spoke "Mr. Desmond Cosby, every day when we come to the Shupavu Building, we come to work with pride, and then work harder with pride. No matter the size of the magnitude, you come to work to win." Then TD cracked a smirk, "The great Reginald F. Lewis once said"

"I have a rule: I never talk about a deal until it's done."

Desmond was stunned for a moment, and then responded, "Mrs. Burn, Mrs. Ursula Burns once said"

"I want to stop transforming and just start being."

..... "And with that being said Mr. Downing, I am part of a dynasty, and I feel like a winner…. And I want to continue to win." Desmond responded with a stern look on his face.

Mr. Downing reached out his hand to shake Dez's hand, and replied, "Great salesmanship, I hear you talking, but I will be closely observing your actions."

Back in New Orleans' headquarter, Diamond awaited for the arrival meeting with business professionals from Jamaica.

All arriving separately, former Jamaica 100 and 200 meter Olympic Medalist, the lovely Jade Simone (Owner of Simone and Company, Acquisition Advisory and Management), Jeremiah Wyclef Hamilton (Owner of Maroon Blue Mountain (MBM) Investments, Private Equity), George Gordon (Owner of Gordon and Associates, Real Estate). Diamond and Kendra swiftly greeted all of them. All seated at the balcony table, Diamond opened up with his objectives.

"Ladies and gentlemen, businesswomen, businessmen, thank you all for coming up to The Big Easy. I am sure you have probably heard rumors or inquired or most likely speculated why I have called you all up here and plans are…. well I am a straightforward type of guy and I think you should all hear from me…. Face to face, business ideas that will bring profitability to Jamaica, no great mystery, yet, mysterious." Diamond stood as he spoke his intro

Diamond continued, "I am an investor, but I don't just invest anymore for more wealth. I invest to create an opportunity for others because there's plenty of money to spread to others."

George Gordon abruptly interrupted, "Mr. Asanti, in all respect, it is capitalism mon, or big bank takes little bank. And you are a big bank compared to us."

Diamond stood there with a calm demeanor as George expressed his business concerns upfront.

"He is very right you know. Rumor is that you have over 400 million dollars en route to Jamaica real estate, Mr. Asanti." Jeremiah Wyclef Hamilton spoke

Ms. Jade Simone sat there waiting for a reaction from Diamond as he listened to a collection of business concerns (and some fears) between Mr. Hamilton and Mr. Gordon. However, Diamond stood there as if he was a soldier in an at-ease stance absorbing the comments.

Diamond then starts using an analogy to make things clearer of his intentions.

"Captain Cudjoe knew what he had to do in order to secure his people freedom as soon as he arrived on land.... Well, on behalf of my father who is a maroon and a chef.... I would like, no, I need to be part of that ingredient that brought Jamaica prosperity and wealth to many more Jamaicans and generations afterward." Diamond spoke

Jade then cracked a smile and responded, "Mr. Asanti...."

"Please, everyone call me Diamond" Diamond immediately responded on clearing up how he would like to be addressed amongst his peers.

"…. So, they say you are a financial crusader, appearing to at least attempt to spread the wealth. My question is what potentials do you see in Jamaica?" Jade asked

"Yes, my intention is to spread the wealth, but only to those who are willing and smart enough to work for it. Freedom of any sort does not come for free. And as for as Jamaica, there's a lot to be done, but it can be done if everybody wants to work for the vision and work together. The Maroons did not become the Maroons overnight." Diamond

"What is your estimated duration of you getting the return on your investment?" Jeremiah

Diamond then sat down in his chair, leaned back with a smile.

"We all know Jamaica is a natural resource of many commodities…. And we also know that Jamaica's economy does not live in Jamaica, therefore Jamaica suffer economically. With that being said, here we are in this meeting…. Jeremiah, currently, I am estimating over a billion in this investment alone. And Jeremiah, Jade and George, I do not want to do this alone, because the world is paying attention. And since I have their attention, let's point it towards Jamaica progressively and constructively." Diamond

"A billion over huh mon? Mi see yuh not scared, wah gwaan." George

"I am listening." Jeremiah

"So am I." Jade

Diamond leaned forward in his chair, resting his arms on the table and begin to lay out his strategy, "First, the land. Quietly. From here on out, less exposure is better. This way we (me and you all) can keep the price affordable for all of us to continue purchasing without drawing attention by other major international investors. My team will be going from North to South and East to West acquiring an unattractive large portion of raw land and water rights and then spread out the buying to popular areas.... Starting tonight."

"And like other major investors, when time gets tuff, are you just going to sell it off, it is Jamaica?" Jade asked

"No, this is hopefully, lifetime term after I am gone.... As I said before, I do not want to do this by myself. Jamaica's children need to see itself growing internally. That is why you all are here, and that is why we are discussing this because you all have plenty of cash on your balance sheet. Once we have enough land, start investing in modernization. Removing the stigma of "The Third World" country while industrializing the island, not depending on tourism, at all. The rise of Jamaica will then start attracting more investor but by that time, you all will be in a position to determine the Asking Price." Diamond

George stood up with enthusiasm "I like it mon, mi fear nah chaka-chaka intention. The rise of Jamaica, yah mon."

Back in China, a bit over an hour and a half before the buyout negotiation's meeting, Raymond is on the phone (getting pointers) from a classmate, a Jamaican private investor from the alma mater of Alcorn State University, Floyd M. Smith.

"Spider, they (Maochow Koutai Company) are looking upward between an instant 4 to 7 percent return on the point of sale. Especially, if the Sasksa (Sasksa Eleankwok, Executive Director of Sales and Purchasing) is doing the most talking. She looks exotic, but trust me, she is very structured, already knows what she wants and does not want any lagniappe. No Lagniappe…. Same way, when it comes to business." Floyd

"Understand brother, no rollercoaster negotiating, just a price." Raymond responded

"You got it mon." Floyd

Raymond then met with Thomas and Desmond to do an adjustment to their buying price.

Later on, less than fifteen minutes before the closing of the bell, Thomas is on the phone with Diamond.

"We got it, 6 million shares at $47, they are happy with their near 10 percent profit on top of another 3 percent of the principal cost. But here is the kicker, shortly after we inked the acquisition deal, a phone call came from London Smirnoff...."

"TD! You are telling me that Deiago already knows about our new position." Diamond

"Word travels fast.... Congratulations, you are now labeled as the modern-day Sneaky Corporate Raider." TD

"Sneaky Corporate Raider? Someone is not going to be on my Christmas List this year." Diamond chuckled

"That's not the real deal, we just bought their shares 3% more than what Deiago would have bidded them for...... I will bet you a $10 bill that Deiago had planned to do an acquisition or merger of their own and needed Maochow's block of shares." TD

"Right, but we just up their buyback price.... and the market will respond crazily." Diamond

"Yes, and look like it will go past $60 a share before we file the 13-D, plus the call options." TD

"Plus the call options!?!" Diamond

Proud as Diamond was of the monetary gain and his team of rainmakers, he decided to...

"Cash-in the call options and have the Yamaye Brewery (Jamaica's Beer Company) cost evaluation by the time you arrive back to the United States.... also let Maochow's representative know that we do not intend to hold after this acquisition." Diamond directed

"Ok, we will make it do what it do sir." TD

The same day, within 2 hours after the Closing of The Bell, the stock soared up to $53 during after-hours trading. Deiago's representative immediately called Shupavu to arrange a meeting between CEOs and Negotiation Staff.

["if I wanted to talk to you, I would have come to you. However, you want to talk to me about business, therefore, you come to me." Diamond spoke]

Three days later, 1 day before the filing of the 13-D, a meeting was arranged at Shupavu's high rise building in the neighborhood of Queensborough, Shreveport, Louisiana, between Shupavu and Deiago's staff. Jade, George, Jeremiah and William "Billy Boyo" Rowe of Lion Spliff Marketing were also in attendance.

After greeting each other in the Shupavu's foyer along with enjoying complimentary Louisiana Hors d'oeuvre, Kendra instructed everyone to go to the conference room and be seated.

"We have come in good fate to parley with Shupavu as I and my board members who are in the teleconference monitor.... we would want to gain a comprehensive meaning of what your intentions are in Deiago. I see that you have business individuals from Jamaica attending this meeting as well. Thank heavens our lawyer is in attendance.... Mr. Asanti, what is your interest in Deiago?" Wolff Greener, Deiago's Chief Executive Officer

"I could be cliché and say "money", but honestly I want a brewery company under Shupavu's banner." Diamond answering Greener question with direct eye contact.

"Deiago was in a pre-stage negotiation with another company involving a merger until we have learned about your new position. And today Mr. Asanti, you are telling us your intention is to take over Deiago International Brewery?" Wolff asks in a near emotional tone

"No need for anyone to get excited, this is just business. I do not wish to file a 13 D on tomorrow because I like your company the way it is, and your semi-annual dividends..... so here are my 2 optional proposals. Mr. Desmond Cosby, will you?" Diamond asked for Dez to announce Shupavu's alternative proposal.

"Ladies and gentlemen, board members of Deiago International Brewery, Shupavu's have prepared the alternative proposal following:

1.   Sell ninety-seven percent (97%) of our block shares starting at $60 down to $57.50, although the street may bid it over $63 once social media gets hold of the filing during open market (Desmond raised his eyebrow as he looked at Deiago's lawyer and board members [in the monitor]);

2.   Or 85% controlling interest in your Yamaye Brewery's Subsidiary, and 97% of our block shares starting $57.50 down to $54."

-   Dez announced

Jade gasp for air and the Jamaican Businessmen begin whispering once they heard Yamaye Brewery in the 2nd proposal. Diamond and London Smirnoff began to make eye to eye contact as if it was a face to face standoff.

[DIAMOND THEN CLEARED HIS THROAT]

"Oh yes, due to Deiago's Chairman, London Smirnoff's comment "Sneaky Corporate Raider" on social media, we have just decided to modify proposal number 2, from "$57.50 down to $54" to "$58.00 down to $55.50"- Dez clarified.

Deiago members understood that if they do not buy Shupavu's shares back at those terms, Diamond will be in a position to hedge any future business of Deiago.

London Smirnoff immediately requested a private phone conference with the Deiago's staff, as direct eye contact and facial expressions between Diamond and London start to intensify.

"By all means." Diamond responded with a stern look.

Inside The Numbers

- Before the meeting, Deiago's stock closed at $54.17 of the U.S. Market

- Shupavu's 11% ownership (16.5 Million shares) of Diago'stock is currently valued at $893.8 Million, (a profit of $233.8 Million)

- Yamaye Brewery Company's Total Value is at a bit over $60 Million

Within two hours of Deiago deliberating with the board members, everyone regrouped back in the conference room to close out the meeting.

"Although, it is too late, Mr. Asanti, I have refuted and redacted my comment on social media…. We understand that your company is elevating smartly and fairly. Therefore, I apologize." London spoke

Jade gave an arousing smirk to Diamond as if she had discovered her male hero.

Wolff then stood up to announce Deiago counteroffer, "Deiago has prepared to relinquish 100% ownership of Yamaye Brewery to Shupavu Investments. Deiago has also prepared to privately buyback of Shupavu's block of shares (16million shares) in Deiago at $56.15 with a disclaimer to disqualify any green mailing activities."

Diamond stood up and walk toward the window overlooking west of Queensborough to Mooretown. He then looked at his assistant, Kendra and nodded his head.

Kendra stood up and responded with a military firm look, "Shupavu accepts your offer."

After shaking hands, Deiago's staff departed with the signed agreement of their offer.

"Shupavu Team, a team of rainmakers, we have made decent money these last 9 days as well as getting 100% ownership in Yamaye Brewery…. Here is to The Rise of Jamaica." Diamond as he raised his glass to a successful acquisition.

"To The Rise of Jamaica" all spoke as a team.

.... Home Brew In Jamaica.......

Series 3, The Rise Of Jamaica,

Coming January 2020